D0566777

PRESENTED TO

PRESENTED BY

DATE

PROVERBS
FOR LIFE™
for
Women

inspirio™

Proverbs for Life™ for Women
ISBN 0-310-80178-8

Copyright © 2003 by GRQ Ink, Inc.
Franklin, Tennessee 37067
"Proverbs for Life" is a trademark owned by GRQ, Inc.

Published by Inspirio™, The gift group of Zondervan
5300 Patterson Avenue, SE
Grand Rapids, Michigan 49530

Requests for information should be addressed to:
Inspirio™, The gift group of Zondervan
Grand Rapids, Michigan 49530
http://www.inspiriogifts.com

Compiler: Lila Empson
Associate Editor: Janice Jacobson
Project Manager: Tom Dean
Manuscript written by Cherie Rayburn of Creative Word in conjunction with
          Snapdragon Editorial Group, Inc.
Design: Whisner Design Group

O BEY THE LORD

AND YOU WILL LIVE A LONG LIFE,

CONTENT AND SAFE FROM HARM.

PROVERBS 19:23 GNT

Contents

Introduction 8

1. No Record (Forgiving Others)............................10

2. Just Rewards (Clean Conscience) 12

3. Giving from the Heart (Charity) 14

4. Happily Will I Follow (God's Direction) 16

5. Pretty Is as Pretty Does (Beauty) 20

6. A Joyful Anticipation (Aging) 22

7. What Cash Can't Buy (Money) 24

8. A Few Soft Words (Anger) 26

9. More Than Enough (Contentment)................30

10. Saying What You Mean (Communication)....32

11. No One Will Ever Know—But Me (Integrity) 34

12. I Quit (Perseverance) 36

13. The Promotion (Disappointment) 40

14. The Lord Is with Me (Overcoming Fear).......42

15. Experience Counts (Parents) 44

16. Did You Know I . . . (Pride) 46

17. God Is Listening (Prayer)..............................50

18. Teach Me to Wait (Patience) 52

19. Being There When It Matters (Dependability) 54

20. Peace Like a River (Peace)..............................56

21. I'm Yours, Lord (Obedience) 60

22. I Can't Believe I Said That (Words) 62

23. Always Unnoticed (Work) 64

24. Enough for Today (Faith)....................................66

25. Hanging On (Preserving Hope) 70

26. No Matter What (Kindness) 72

27. Guarding Your Health (Wellness) 74

28. A Righteous Cause (Justice) 76

29. The Rumor Stops Here (Gossip)...................80

30. A Good Name (Reputation) 82

31. Going On (Mistakes) 84

32. The Lord Gives Me Strength (Growing Strong) 86

33. Making It Big (Success) 90

34. Wise Solutions (Common Sense)...................92

35. Hands Extended (Hospitality) 94

36. Back to the Books (Exercising Your Mind) 96

37. The Real Reason (Motives) 100

38. I'm Happy for You (Jealousy) 102

39. It's a Choice (Cheerfulness) 104

40. I'll Get to It Later (Diligence) 106

41. Straight Talk (Friendship) 110

42. Turning the Other Cheek (Revenge)...............112

43. Clean Before the Lord (Holiness) 114

44. Knowing What to Do (Advice) 116

45. An Uplifting Word (Encouragement) 120

46. Thinking to Win (Thoughts) 122

Introduction

The book of Proverbs contains the timeless wisdom each person needs to live a happy, healthy, well-balanced life. Each entry in this book teaches a practical principle designed to encourage good choices and positive problem solving.

Proverbs for Life™ for Women takes those valuable principles and applies them to the issues women care about most, such as beauty, money, commitment, health, and hospitality. As you read through these pages, may you find the practical answers—God's answers—to the questions you are asking.

Charm is deceptive, and beauty fleeting; but a woman who fears the LORD is to be praised.

— Proverbs 31:30 NIV

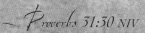

The Virtuous Woman

Mortals, who would follow me,

Love virtue, she alone is free;

She can teach you how to climb

Higher than the spherey clime;

Or if virtue feeble were,

Heaven itself would stoop to her.

John Milton

No Record

If you want people to like you, forgive them when they wrong you.

— Proverbs 17:9 GNT

Human beings are flawed. It's that simple. At some time, in some way, each and every person we love and trust will fail us. It isn't a question of if but when. That's why it is so important to decide in advance how you will respond when the sting of a wrong leaves its mark on your heart.

Conventional wisdom says to get even, but godly wisdom says that happiness, peace, reconciliation, and love will follow you when you do just the opposite—cover an offense with love and forgiveness.

That doesn't mean it's always right to ignore such actions or the motives that drive them. But it does mean that it's right to refuse to broadcast it, nag about it, or use it to gain power over the offender.

When you cover an offense, you acknowledge that you also are flawed and in need of forgiveness. You allow the law of love to rule over the law of retribution in your life.

Wouldn't it be great to live in a world where you never had to experience the pain of betrayal, where no one ever said hurtful things to you or failed you in any way? Unfortunately, it would be a world without people, because people aren't perfect. It would also be a world without the touch of human kindness, because you would have no need to forgive, and it would be a world without love, because forgiveness is the wick that keeps love's flame burning.

Love does not keep a record of wrongs.

I Corinthians 13:5
GNT

Try this: *When you've suffered an offense, write down your feelings on a piece of paper. Then seal it in an unlabeled envelope and pray about it every day until you feel you know what action, if any, God wants you to take. When you are at peace with your response, burn or shred the envelope without opening it.*

Love forgives all offenses.

Proverbs 10:12
GNT

Every person should have a special cemetery lot in which to bury the faults of friends and loved ones.

Author Unknown

11

Just Rewards

The LORD gave us mind and conscience; we cannot hide from ourselves.
— *Proverbs 20:27* GNT

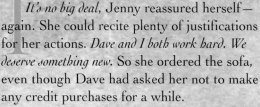

It's no big deal, Jenny reassured herself— again. She could recite plenty of justifications for her actions. *Dave and I both work hard. We deserve something new.* So she ordered the sofa, even though Dave had asked her not to make any credit purchases for a while.

By the time she got home, Jenny's conscience was bothering her. She fought back with a barrage of excuses, but her excuses couldn't still the nagging voice inside. For three nights, she lay awake, tossing and turning. Daytime was even worse. She was forgetful, preoccupied, and unproductive. How could such a little thing be such a big problem?

Jenny finally acknowledged that her decision had shown a true lack of concern for her husband's wishes and their financial welfare and that her decision did not honor God. She called the store to stop the delivery. *Why did I wait so long to do the right thing?* she asked herself.

Peace of mind and a clear conscience are precious commodities, and they cannot be bought for any price. They are yours only when you determine day by day, hour by hour, minute by minute to do the right thing no matter what. Doing the right thing is basic to honesty, integrity, and righteousness. When you fall short—as everyone does—God has provided a remedy. He is quick to forgive you when you ask and to restore you to peace and well-being.

Try this: Most poor choices are made spontaneously, so adopt the twenty-four-hour rule. When you feel a twinge of conscience, wait twenty-four hours before acting or speaking, no matter how justified the action or words might seem. Pray and wait until your heart and your head are in agreement, and then don't hesitate to do what you know is right.

KEEP YOUR FAITH AND A CLEAR CONSCIENCE.

1 TIMOTHY 1:19 GNT

TO DO WHAT IS RIGHT AND JUST IS MORE ACCEPTABLE TO THE LORD THAN SACRIFICE.

PROVERBS 21:3 NIV

Conscience tells us in our innermost being of the presence of God and of the moral difference between good and evil.

BILLY GRAHAM

Giving from the Heart

Be generous, and you will be prosperous. Help others, and you will be helped.

~ *Proverbs 11:25* GNT

What I kept, I lost. What I spent, I had. What I gave, I have.
—Ancient Proverb

Settling into her seat at the memorial service, Karen closed her eyes and focused on recalling her Aunt Joan's kind and loving face. She had been a truly remarkable woman. And when people began to stand up and speak, Karen realized just how remarkable—and generous—her aunt had been.

Karen learned that her beloved aunt had made regular contributions from her meager pension and savings to her local church, several foreign missionaries, and a nearby homeless shelter. Her aunt had also donated homemade jams and homegrown vegetables to the local food bank.

One by one, the people whose lives Karen's aunt had touched told their stories with glistening eyes. It was obvious that her aunt had received a rich return for her generosity—a bounty of love, respect, joy, and friendship.

Though she might not express her generosity in the same way, Karen resolved to learn from her aunt's godly example.

Karen's Aunt Joan understood the powerful principle of giving. She knew that sharing what she had with others was like seeding the clouds above her head and releasing showers of blessing into her life. She lived what she believed. Even after she left this world, the cycle of blessing that she had initiated continued to flow among those whose lives she had touched. The way to begin tapping in to these showers of blessings is simply to start seeding the clouds and start sharing from your own abundant blessings.

Try this: *On index cards, plan a specific act of charity—such as volunteering at a food bank or visiting a nursing home—each week for eight weeks. Map out these activities in detail at the beginning of the eight-week period. After each activity, record your thoughts and comments on the back of the card.*

GOOD THINGS WILL COME TO THOSE WHO ARE WILLING TO LEND FREELY.

PSALM 112:5 NIRV

ANYONE WHO IS KIND TO POOR PEOPLE LENDS TO THE LORD.

PROVERBS 19:17 NIRV

The truly generous is the truly wise, and he who loves not others, lives unblest.

HENRY HOME

Happily Will I Follow

Remember the LORD in everything you do, and he will show you the right way.

— Proverbs 3:6 GNT

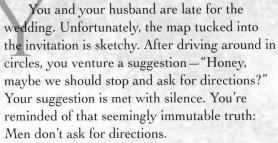

You and your husband are late for the wedding. Unfortunately, the map tucked into the invitation is sketchy. After driving around in circles, you venture a suggestion—"Honey, maybe we should stop and ask for directions?" Your suggestion is met with silence. You're reminded of that seemingly immutable truth: Men don't ask for directions.

That "truth" has found its way into many jokes. But before laughing at men, step back and consider your own actions. As a woman you may be more apt to ask for road directions, but how often do you neglect to seek direction for the journey of life?

It's possible to think you know exactly where you're going, only to find that you missed a turn in your career or your relationship, and now you're completely lost. It's good to remember that you need to stop often, check in with God, and make sure that you're going his way, which is always the right way!

It would be great if life came with a detailed set of directions. You would always know the best route to take. You would always know which detours and side roads to avoid. But then you wouldn't need to have a close relationship with God. God wants you to grow close to him and to develop faith in him to provide direction for your life. He created you, he knows you, he loves you—and he will never steer you wrong! Is God directing your journey?

Try this: When you go somewhere in your car, say a little prayer of thanks to God each time you make a turn on the way to your destination. Thank him for always being there to provide you with direction and to show you the way to negotiate life's every turn.

WHOEVER GIVES HEED TO INSTRUCTION PROSPERS.

PROVERBS 16:20 NIV

I HAVE TAUGHT YOU WISDOM AND THE RIGHT WAY TO LIVE. NOTHING WILL STAND IN YOUR WAY IF YOU WALK WISELY, AND YOU WILL NOT STUMBLE WHEN YOU RUN.

PROVERBS 4:11–12 GNT

It is morally impossible to exercise trust in God while there is failure to wait upon Him for guidance and direction.

D. E. HOSTE

The Godly Woman

I beseech Thee now, my Savior,

Make me more like Thee,

Pure of word and action

May I Thy servant be.

In this way, my Savior,

I pray the world will see

A lot more of Thy goodness

And a great deal less of me.

Andrea Garney

*If you do what is right,
you are certain to be
rewarded.*

~ *Proverbs* 11:18 GNT

*Spiritual exercise is
valuable in every way,
because it promises life
both for the present and
for the future.*

~ *1 Timothy* 4:8 GNT

GODLINESS IS
GLORY IN THE
SEED, AND GLORY
IS GODLINESS IN
THE FLOWER.

WILLIAM GURNALL

Pretty Is as Pretty Does

Charm is deceptive and beauty disappears, but a woman who honors the LORD should be praised.

— Proverbs 31:30 GNT

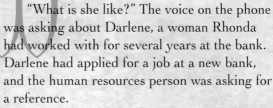

"What is she like?" The voice on the phone was asking about Darlene, a woman Rhonda had worked with for several years at the bank. Darlene had applied for a job at a new bank, and the human resources person was asking for a reference.

A picture of Darlene popped into Rhonda's mind. Darlene was rather average looking, if judged by commercial standards, and she weighed more than her fashion-conscious sisters. Her hairstyle was simple, as was her clothing. Yet her laughter overrode trendy considerations. She took pride in doing her job well, and she always had time to help other tellers when they ran into snags. She was the first to volunteer for bank charity projects, and the line of patrons at her window was always the longest.

"Darlene is a beautiful person," Rhonda replied. Darlene's resignation would leave a void that not just anyone could fill. "Yes, she is a beautiful person."

20

Rhonda absorbed a valuable spiritual truth through her acquaintance with Darlene: Real beauty comes from the inside. A simple concept, yes, but everything in this multimedia-saturated society teaches just the opposite. Each year, women in the United States spend millions of dollars on blushes and shadows and lotions and perfumes in an effort to be more beautiful on the outside. But for Rhonda—and for you—the wonder is that inner beauty comes from a close walk with God.

Try this: Think about the most beautiful woman in your life—the one whose inner beauty radiates light and joy wherever she goes. Jot down the specific traits that make her beautiful. Then make a point during this week to thank her for at least one of those traits and for being an example of true beauty to you.

THE LORD SAID, "[PEOPLE] LOOK AT THE OUTWARD APPEARANCE, BUT I LOOK AT THE HEART."

1 SAMUEL 16:7 GNT

IT IS YOUR OWN FACE THAT YOU SEE REFLECTED IN THE WATER AND IT IS YOUR OWN SELF THAT YOU SEE IN YOUR HEART.

PROVERBS 27:19 GNT

Good in the heart works its way up into the face and prints its own beauty there.

AUTHOR UNKNOWN

A Joyful Anticipation

Gray hair is a crown of splendor; it is attained by a righteous life.

— *Proverbs 16:31 NIV*

Jeanne had just received the news—in six months she was going to be a grandmother. She was ecstatic, but at the same time, it felt a little odd that she was actually old enough to have a grandchild.

Jeanne pulled the family album off the bookshelf to add some pages, because she planned to take lots of pictures of the baby. She found all her favorite, familiar images in the album, including the one of herself as a little girl sitting on her grandmother's lap. Memories of the times they had spent together baking cookies, playing go fish, and sharing Bible stories flooded back.

Suddenly, Jeanne saw herself in that old photo, this time as the grandmother with her precious grandchild-to-be on her lap. She knew at that moment that she wanted to be a grandmother like the one that God had blessed her with. And she was glad that God had given her the joyful anticipation of grandparenthood.

🌿 It's a fact. Every day you wake up, you're older than the day before. But the fact that your body has grown a day older doesn't necessarily mean that your mind and spirit have, at the same time, grown a day wiser and more mature. That's because growing physically older requires only that you exist from one day to the next. But growing spiritually requires that you strive to follow Christ constantly, daily. Each morning is an opportunity to wake up better and wiser, and not merely older.

🌿 *Try this: Greeting cards often make light of growing older, and they sometimes put down rather than lift up the person who receives them. Consider buying a box of attractive informal cards and writing your own greetings that celebrate the special joys, blessings, and insights that come with aging.*

OBEY THE LORD AND YOU WILL LIVE LONGER.

PROVERBS 10:27 GNT

WISDOM WILL ADD YEARS TO YOUR LIFE.

PROVERBS 9:11 GNT

To know how to grow old is the master work of wisdom and one of the most difficult chapters in the great art of living.

HENRI-FRÉDÉRIC AMIEL

What Cash Can't Buy

Those who depend on their wealth will fall like the leaves of autumn, but the righteous will prosper like the leaves of summer.

— *Proverbs* 11:28 GNT

Nothing that is God's can be obtained with money.
—Tertullian

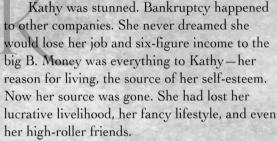

Kathy was stunned. Bankruptcy happened to other companies. She never dreamed she would lose her job and six-figure income to the big B. Money was everything to Kathy—her reason for living, the source of her self-esteem. Now her source was gone. She had lost her lucrative livelihood, her fancy lifestyle, and even her high-roller friends.

Kathy began to spend more time with her family—specifically, her sister Mary and Mary's husband and two boys. She found herself at her sister's house for dinner most evenings and at the park with her nephews most Saturdays. She also got involved in the family's church, where she learned that true self-esteem comes from a relationship with God.

Eventually, Kathy found a new job. The salary was only a third of what she had made before, but that no longer mattered to her so much. She had learned that there are some things—such as love and a real purpose in life—that money can't buy.

It's both reassuring and exciting to learn firsthand, as Kathy did, that God does indeed prosper the righteous—despite occasional appearances to the contrary in this materialistic society. When your confidence plummets, your situation looks dire, and you don't know which way to turn, you can know without doubt that God will take care of you and supply all your needs in ways you may not be able to predict. Put your trust in God and stay in constant touch with God through prayer and his Word.

TRY THIS: *Write yourself a check. On the "pay to" line, write your name. On the amount line, write the right attitude toward money. On the signature line, write God. Leave the check in your checkbook. Every time you write another check, let it remind you to keep the value you place on money in line with God's values.*

IF YOU LONG TO BE RICH, YOU WILL NEVER GET ALL YOU WANT.

ECCLESIASTES 5:10 GNT

BE WISE ENOUGH NOT TO WEAR YOURSELF OUT TRYING TO GET RICH.

PROVERBS 23:4 GNT

If you want to feel rich, just count all the things you have that money can't buy.

AUTHOR UNKNOWN

A Few Soft Words

A gentle answer quiets anger, but a harsh one stirs it up.

~ Proverbs 15:1 GNT

No doubt about it, Mr. Burns was a difficult patient. He had every nurse on the second floor scared even to deliver his food.

When it was time to take Mr. Burns's vitals, Sandy, who had just transferred to the second floor from ICU, volunteered for the job. She had attended Mr. Burns two weeks earlier when he had been brought in following a serious car accident, which his wife hadn't survived.

When Sandy entered Room 212, the other nurses listened for the inevitable tirade. Unlike the other nurses, however, when Mr. Burns began to wave his arms and shout at her to leave, she stood her ground.

"I know what it's like to lose someone you love—how unfair it seems. God knows too. Please let us help you." Mr. Burns at first stared at her. Then without a word, he offered her his arm so she could do her job.

Sandy was the carrier of a contagious condition—kindness. Her empathy for Mr. Burns and his tragic loss broke through his wall of anger. Just as firefighters usually don't fight fire with more fire, as a Christian, you should shy from responding to anger with more anger. Make it your goal to be a carrier of kindness. You will welcome the healing that comes with gentleness and kindness.

The words of good people are wise, and they are always fair.

Psalm 37:30 GNT

Human anger does not achieve God's righteous purpose.

James 1:20 GNT

Try this: *Think about a time you responded to anger with anger. Play the conversation again in your mind, and think about the point when you could have responded with kindness. Do you think the conversation would have gone differently if you had? Ask the Lord to forgive you for that incident and to help you respond next time with a soft answer.*

If you are patient in one moment of anger, you will avoid one hundred days of sorrow.

Ancient Proverb

The Loving Woman

Love is an attitude—
love is a prayer,
For a soul in sorrow,
a heart in despair.
She seeks not her own
at expense of another.
Love reaches God
when it reaches your brother.

Author Unknown

Let love and faithfulness never leave you; bind them around your neck.

~ *Proverbs 3:3* NIV

There is no fear in love; perfect love drives out all fear.

~ *1 John 4:18* GNT

LOVE IS THE SUM
OF ALL VIRTUE,
AND LOVE
DISPOSES US
TO DO GOOD.

JONATHAN EDWARDS

More than Enough

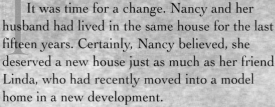

Let me be neither rich nor poor. So give me only as much food as I need. If I have more, I might say that I do not need you. But if I am poor, I might steal and bring disgrace on my God.

— *Proverbs* 30:8–9 GNT

A little is as much as a lot, if it is enough.
—Steve Brown

It was time for a change. Nancy and her husband had lived in the same house for the last fifteen years. Certainly, Nancy believed, she deserved a new house just as much as her friend Linda, who had recently moved into a model home in a new development.

Nancy called a Realtor, who completed the paperwork and placed a big FOR SALE sign in front of her house. The Realtor later called Nancy to read an ad she had written for the newspaper. Nancy pictured her house as the Realtor described a sunny kitchen with lots of counter space, a cozy family room with a fireplace, and a spacious backyard with big shade trees. Nancy was surprised. It was as if she were seeing her house for the first time.

Suddenly she interrupted the Realtor, "I've changed my mind. I don't want to sell. I never realized how wonderful this house really is and how contented I am living right here!"

Contentment and gratitude come with the right perspective. As a citizen of the world's richest country, you are incredibly blessed. Consider this—one-fifth of the world's population (1.2 billion people) live on less than one dollar a day in conditions of almost unimaginable suffering and want. In fact, your garbage disposal eats better than one-third of your neighbors around the globe. God has enriched your life with more than you need. How does your life rate on the contentment scale?

Try this: Volunteer at an organization, either through your church or through a civic group, that works for and serves the poor. Cooking and serving in a soup kitchen or working at a food or clothing pantry will remind you how fortunate you are and fill you with gratitude for everything God has given you.

Better a little with the fear of the Lord than great wealth with turmoil.

Proverbs 15:16 NIV

Keep your lives free from the love of money, and be satisfied with what you have.

Hebrews 13:5 GNT

Contentment is a pearl of great price, and whoever procures it at the expense of ten thousand desires makes a wise and a happy purchase.

John Balguy

Saying What You Mean

A word aptly spoken is like apples of gold in settings of silver.

— *Proverbs 25:11 NIV*

OUR WORDS ARE
A FAITHFUL INDEX
OF THE STATE OF
OUR SOULS.
—SAINT FRANCIS
DE SALES

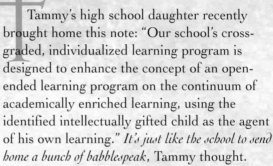

Tammy's high school daughter recently brought home this note: "Our school's cross-graded, individualized learning program is designed to enhance the concept of an open-ended learning program on the continuum of academically enriched learning, using the identified intellectually gifted child as the agent of his own learning." *It's just like the school to send home a bunch of babblespeak*, Tammy thought.

When she thought more about it, Tammy realized that babblespeak is common in many realms of life. In fact, Tammy recalled that when she started attending church a year ago, she was confused by much of the Christianese. She learned firsthand that Christians are as guilty of using babblespeak as anyone. Many simple concepts—such as salvation from sin and the role of God's Spirit in a believer's life—were presented to her in ways that were hard to decipher. She wondered, *How do such beautiful, straightforward truths get turned into such gibberish?*

꙰ When Jesus shared a complicated spiritual concept, he simplified it by wrapping it into a story. Jesus' stories were about everyday situations his listeners could relate to—wedding banquets, wayward children, vineyards. His stories were simple and clear, and the lessons behind them unforgettable. As with everything else in life, Jesus is the model of effective communication. He teaches that the best way to relate to others is by tapping into your common experience as a human being.

꙰ TRY THIS: *Briefly write out what you believe. Circle any words or phrases you think might be unclear to a nonbeliever. Think of ways to explain their meaning that are simple and clear. This activity is not an easy one, but it will make your words a more powerful tool for communicating the love of God to others.*

YOUR SPEECH SHOULD ALWAYS BE PLEASANT AND INTERESTING.

COLOSSIANS 4:6 GNT

WHEN WISE PEOPLE SPEAK, THEY MAKE KNOWLEDGE ATTRACTIVE.

PROVERBS 15:2 GNT

Be humble and gentle in your conversation; and of few words, I charge you; but always pertinent when you speak.

WILLIAM PENN

No One Will Ever Know—But Me

Honest people are safe and secure.

— *Proverbs* 10:9 GNT

It was a perfect day for their dinosaur outing. Karen's sons, five-year-old Phillip and eleven-year-old Jason, were dinosaur fanatics, and Karen was taking them to a *T. rex* exhibit at the museum. From there they were on their way to a 3-D dinosaur movie.

Unfortunately, at the museum, a sign read children under the age of six were not allowed into the exhibit. She hesitated, but only briefly. Karen took the boys aside and instructed them to tell the ticket agent that Phillip was six.

After a wonderful time at the exhibit, they went to the theater, where Karen discovered another sign. This one read kids under ten were admitted at half price. Once again, she coached the boys, this time to say that Jason was nine.

Later that night, as the boys were getting ready for bed, Karen stopped outside their door, listening as they excitedly recalled the day's events. She froze in shame when Phillip said, "Jason, how old are we? I'm really confused."

Sometimes so-called little sins have big consequences. Karen's no-big-deal lapse of integrity cost her credibility as a role model to her sons. Humans suffer periodic integrity lapses. That's why you've been given a conscience. Your conscience sounds a clear warning when you're veering off the integrity track. Pay attention to that small voice. It is a true gift from God!

Try this: Soak a sponge with water. Now press on it. What happens? Consider that your life is like a sponge—soaked through, not with water, but with the character of Christ. Then whenever any pressure is applied, such as the pressure to compromise your integrity, the character of Christ will flow out, enabling you to overcome the impulse to sin.

The integrity of the upright shall guide them.

Proverbs 11:3 KJV

May integrity and uprightness protect me, because my hope is in you, Lord.

Psalm 25:21 NIV

It is obvious that to be in earnest in seeking the truth is an indispensable requisite for finding it.

John Henry Newman

i Quit

The longings of people who work hard are completely satisfied.

— *Proverbs 13:4 NIRV*

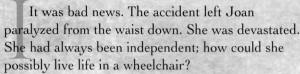

I It was bad news. The accident left Joan paralyzed from the waist down. She was devastated. She had always been independent; how could she possibly live life in a wheelchair?

At the rehabilitation center, Joan met others in similar situations. She was impressed by those who, despite great disabilities, had a positive attitude, smiled, and encouraged others. She earnestly prayed for God's help to be like them.

Emotionally and physically, it was three steps forward, two steps back for Joan. But finally, her determination and faith paid off.

When she was discharged from the rehabilitation center, Joan was able to live alone, cook her meals, do the laundry, and with hand controls even drive a car. After a few months she returned to the architectural firm where she had worked before the accident.

Recently, Joan received a prestigious award from the National Association of Professional Architects. She's looking forward to rolling her wheelchair onto the stage to accept it.

꧁ Joan is an ordinary person who accomplished an extraordinary feat. She did this by committing to overcome her disability, seeking God's help, and sticking by her commitment. Life is filled with commitments, some easy to keep (the commitment to meet with the women's book club every month, for instance) and some difficult (the commitment to tithe). Big or small, easy or difficult, God wants you to keep your commitments. Fortunately, you can always count on him to give you the strength and perseverance to do so.

꧁ TRY THIS: *Many inspiring women throughout history were also ordinary people committed to a cause. How many can you name? Is there a woman in your own life who has accomplished extraordinary things through sheer, determined perseverance? Invite her to lunch and interview her about her secret to sticking with a commitment.*

WHEN I AM READY TO GIVE UP, GOD KNOWS WHAT I SHOULD DO.

PSALM 142:3 GNT

LET US NOT BE WEARY IN WELL DOING: FOR IN DUE SEASON WE SHALL REAP, IF WE FAINT NOT.

GALATIANS 6:9 KJV

Unless commitment is made, there are only promises and hopes . . . but no plans.

PETER DRUCKER

The Spirit-Filled Woman

The life that counts must aim to rise

Above the earth to sunlit skies;

Must fix its gaze on Paradise—

That is the life that counts.

The life that counts must helpful be;

That cares and needs of others see;

Must seek the slave of sin to free—

That is the life that counts.

Author Unknown

Jesus said, "The words I
have spoken to you are
spirit and they are life."

— John 6:63 NIV

In the way of
righteousness there is
life; along that path is
immortality.

— Proverbs 28:25 NIV

I ASKED GOD FOR
ALL THINGS, THAT I
MIGHT ENJOY LIFE.
GOD GAVE ME
LIFE, THAT I MIGHT
ENJOY ALL THINGS.

AUTHOR UNKNOWN

The Promotion

A longing fulfilled is a tree of life.

— *Proverbs 13:12 NIV*

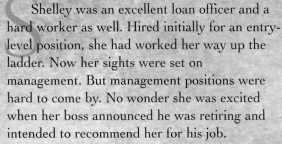

Shelley was an excellent loan officer and a hard worker as well. Hired initially for an entry-level position, she had worked her way up the ladder. Now her sights were set on management. But management positions were hard to come by. No wonder she was excited when her boss announced he was retiring and intended to recommend her for his job.

Shelley spent the next few weeks rehearsing how she would handle her new responsibilities, what she would do with her raise, and even how she would decorate her office. Then the bank president announced that a coworker was being given the promotion. Shelley was overwhelmed with disappointment.

At first she found it difficult to support her new boss. But after much prayer, she put her disappointment behind her and determined to continue to do her best. By the time she moved into management three years later, Shelley realized she had gained the respect of her colleagues and the confidence she needed to do well.

Overcoming life's disappointments is difficult. Shelley could have let anger and resentment make her miserable and spoil what she had worked so hard to achieve. But she chose instead to let it go and move on. When you suffer a disappointment, give it to God and trust him to help you grow from your experience. Work to maintain a good attitude. In this way, you will gain the respect of others—and, most important, you will gain respect for yourself and God's perfect work in your life.

Try this: *Purchase a helium balloon. When you get home, write down on a small piece of paper any disappointments you are having trouble releasing. Attach it to the string and then release the balloon to float away into the heavens. As you meet new disappointments, visualize that balloon carrying them away as well. Then thank God for the opportunity to begin again.*

WISE PEOPLE WALK THE ROAD THAT LEADS UPWARD TO LIFE.

PROVERBS 15:24 GNT

WE KNOW THAT IN ALL THINGS GOD WORKS FOR GOOD WITH THOSE WHO LOVE HIM.

ROMANS 8:28 GNT

Faith is often strengthened right at the place of disappointment.

RODNEY MCBRIDE

The Lord Is with Me

The LORD will keep you safe.

— *Proverbs* 3:26 GNT

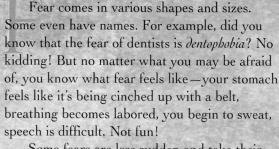

Fear comes in various shapes and sizes. Some even have names. For example, did you know that the fear of dentists is *dentophobia*? No kidding! But no matter what you may be afraid of, you know what fear feels like—your stomach feels like it's being cinched up with a belt, breathing becomes labored, you begin to sweat, speech is difficult. Not fun!

Some fears are less sudden and take their toll over the long haul—like the fear of losing your children, failing in your marriage, losing your job, or not being loved. If it can be encountered in life, it can be feared.

Fear can completely dominate a person's life, and for many that's the case. When fear rises up—reach out and take God's hand. Fear cannot remain in the presence of God. Place your confidence in him, and you can safely navigate any situation life has to offer.

HALF OUR FEARS
ARE BASELESS,
THE OTHER HALF
DISCREDITABLE.
—Christian
Nestell Bovee

Fear is not necessarily bad. In fact, God gave you the emotion of fear. It's your misunderstanding of fear's purpose and lack of faith to deal with it that can get you into trouble. Simply put, fear's function is to warn you of danger, not make you afraid to face it. When fear haunts you, recognize the danger that it represents, then put your faith into full gear to face it. It takes practice, but as your faith glows brighter, you will feel yourself being empowered to deal with it. That's God's promise.

Try this: Fear can be a weight on your spirit, keeping you from being the best you can be. The next time you do a household chore, wear a backpack with something heavy in it, like a dictionary. See how the extra weight slows you down. Then ask God to help you remember to give him the weight of all your fears.

WHOEVER LISTENS TO [WISDOM] WILL LIVE IN SAFETY AND BE AT EASE, WITHOUT FEAR OF HARM.

PROVERBS 1:33 NIV

BE STRONG AND DON'T BE AFRAID! GOD IS COMING TO YOUR RESCUE.

ISAIAH 35:4 GNT

Many of our fears are tissue paper thin, and a single courageous step would carry us through them.

BRENDAN FRANCIS

Experience Counts

Listen to your father; without him you would not exist. When your mother is old, show her your appreciation.

— Proverbs 23:22 GNT

Whatever else you get, get insight.
—Proverbs 4:7 GNT

The kids were driving Janelle crazy. Refusing to eat, jumping on the beds, and fighting, they had pushed her to the edge. Finally Janelle called her mother and asked for help.

The two women met at the coffee shop where, between tears, Janelle poured out her parenting concerns and frustrations. She was surprised when her mother pulled a worn notebook out of her purse and gave it to her. It contained bits of advice her mother had collected and jotted down years back when she was raising Janelle and her siblings. It included all kinds of wise suggestions, such as ways to keep children occupied on car trips, how to deal with temper tantrums, and tips on how to handle sibling rivalry. There were also scripture verses to help fortify her resolve, and her mother's prayers for God's help.

Janelle was struck by the wisdom her mother had gained from God over the years. She knew she had a lot to learn from her.

It's a truth you will recognize. When you were a child you thought your parents knew everything. When you were an adolescent, you thought they knew nothing. By the time you became an adult, you probably realized just how much wisdom your parents accumulated over the years. Your parents are a source of great insight and common sense. Take the time to tap into it. Ask them to share their wisdom with you. It has much value for you and your present efforts.

Try this: The next time you have a problem you would normally discuss with a friend, talk to one of your parents instead. If your parents are no longer living or if their health or other situation prohibits you from being able to speak with them, talk to an older person whom you respect. See what kind of difference "wisdom of the years" lends to your discussion.

To get wisdom is to love oneself.

Proverbs 19:8 NRSV

Keep your father's commands and do not forsake your mother's teaching.

Proverbs 6:20 NIV

The relationship of parent and child remains indelible and indestructible, the strongest relationship on earth.

Theodor Reik

Did You Know I . . .

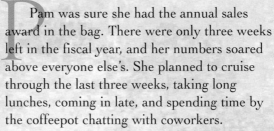

Humility comes before honor.
~ *Proverbs* 18:12 NIV

Pam was sure she had the annual sales award in the bag. There were only three weeks left in the fiscal year, and her numbers soared above everyone else's. She planned to cruise through the last three weeks, taking long lunches, coming in late, and spending time by the coffeepot chatting with coworkers.

Pam wasn't shy about letting others know what an award-winning job she had done. "Sales just fall into my lap," she said, and she talked openly about her plans for the bonus she was going to receive.

Imagine Pam's shock when it was announced that the Salesperson of the Year award was going to Leslie! It seems that over the past three weeks, while Pam was hanging out at the coffeepot, Leslie had continued to plug away, following up all the leads Pam had ignored. An embarrassed Pam congratulated Leslie, and told herself she would avoid pride's trap the next time.

Throughout most of history, the seven deadly sins—pride, envy, anger, sloth, greed, gluttony, and lust—have been a popular subject. Pride is labeled the worst of the seven deadly sins. That's because pride replaces God in a person's life with his or her own self-centered, self-approving thoughts. It is the very trait that got Lucifer thrown out of heaven. Pride is a serious offense to God. If you notice it stalking you, be ever vigilant to keep it out of your heart and mind.

Try this: Pride is like a weed. Its roots grow deep and strong. You can try pulling it up, but if you don't get the roots, the weed will grow back. The next time you feel pride tugging at you, go out and find a few weeds to uproot. Then ask God to help you remove pride from your life—all the way down to its roots.

If you harden your heart with pride, you soften your brain with it too.

Ancient Proverb

The God-Fearing Woman

O taste and see that the Lord is good;

Happy are those who take refuge in him.

O fear the Lord, you his holy ones,

For those who fear him have no want.

The young lions suffer want and hunger,

But those who seek the Lord

Lack no good thing.

Psalm 34:8-10 NRSV

*Respect for the LORD
is like a fountain that
gives life.*

~ Proverbs 14:27 NIRV

*The fear of the LORD is
the beginning of wisdom.*

~ Proverbs 9:10 NIV

THE REMARKABLE

THING ABOUT

FEARING GOD IS

THAT WHEN YOU

FEAR GOD

YOU FEAR

NOTHING ELSE.

OSWALD CHAMBERS

GOD IS LISTENING

When good people pray, the LORD listens.

~ *Proverbs* 15:29 GNT

Even children know what to do in an emergency: Head for the telephone, pick up the receiver, and dial 911. When someone dials 911, the call goes to a dispatcher, who is sitting in front of a computer screen on which the incoming phone number is displayed, along with the street address and the name of the person under whom the phone number is listed.

Paramedics, along with the police and fire departments, are connected to the call automatically. It doesn't matter if the person calling is too upset to be coherent. The dispatcher has all the information necessary to send help immediately. Usually, while the phone call is still going on, the dispatcher is alerting all the needed personnel.

Through dialing this one number, the person calling has immediate access to skills, training, and equipment necessary to turn desperation into hope. Communication is sure and dependable, and the caller knows that help is on the way.

꧁ Prayer is your 911 line to God. It doesn't matter if you know how to articulate your problem to him. He is listening every hour of every day; he knows your name; he understands your circumstance; and he has already dispatched the help you need. You can approach God's throne whenever you desire and pour out your heart to him. Prayer is a precious opportunity that is available 24/7—take advantage of it as often as you can. What a tremendous privilege!

꧁ TRY THIS: *Don't let the fear of doing or saying something wrong keep you from prayer. Try setting an empty chair in front of you. Now imagine that Jesus is sitting in this chair and the two of you are simply having a conversation. The time goes by quickly when you share your heart with your best friend.*

HEAR MY CRY, O GOD; LISTEN TO MY PRAYER.

PSALM 61:1 NIV

DEVOTE YOURSELVES TO PRAYER.

COLOSSIANS 4:2 NIV

Nothing is too great and nothing is too small to commit into the hands of the Lord.

A. W. PINK

Teach Me to Wait

It is better to be patient than powerful.

— *Proverbs* 16:32 GNT

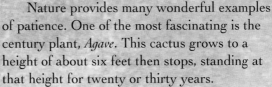

Nature provides many wonderful examples of patience. One of the most fascinating is the century plant, *Agave.* This cactus grows to a height of about six feet then stops, standing at that height for twenty or thirty years.

After that long period of time, a new bud suddenly sprouts at the top of the cactus and grows at a phenomenal rate—up to seven inches a day! The cactus grows to a height of twenty to forty feet, and, finally, a crown of glorious yellow blossoms emerges at the top.

Your life is like the century plant. Often, it is after years of patience and preparation that the most wonderful things happen. All you need do is continue walking with the Lord faithfully, patiently, every day.

Unlike the blooms on a century plant, the crown awaiting us will not be gone in three short weeks. It will last for all eternity!

The path of the Christian life is a long journey with many unexpected turns, delays, and setbacks. Progress can be difficult. It is likely that you are the one who gets the most impatient with your progress. At those times when you're impatient, keep in mind that becoming all that God created you to be takes time—lots of time! But if you keep your eye on the goal, you'll get there—not through your own strength and resources, but through his.

Try this: Make a list of things in life that require patience. Pearls take time to form, but what a beautiful result. Chocolate soufflés also take time, but anyone who has tasted a spoonful knows—it's worth the effort! Now say a prayer, thanking God that he is taking time to mold you into something much more valuable, the image of his Son.

Patience brings peace.

Proverbs 15:18 GNT

If we hope for what we do not yet have, we wait for it patiently.

Romans 8:25 NIV

Only with winter patience can we bring the deep-desired, long-awaited spring.

Anne Morrow Lindbergh

Being There When It Matters

Friends always show their love.

— *Proverbs* 17:17 GNT

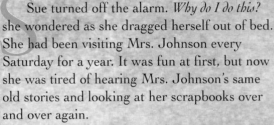

S Sue turned off the alarm. *Why do I do this?* she wondered as she dragged herself out of bed. She had been visiting Mrs. Johnson every Saturday for a year. It was fun at first, but now she was tired of hearing Mrs. Johnson's same old stories and looking at her scrapbooks over and over again.

As she drove to the nursing home, Sue resolved to call the volunteer agency the next week and resign her commitment. A year was long enough—she'd already outlasted most volunteers.

When she arrived at the nursing home, Sue learned that Mrs. Johnson was not well. In fact, the staff predicted that she would not live through the day. When Sue entered Mrs. Johnson's room, the old woman smiled and grabbed her hand, saying weakly, "I knew you would come." Sue, ashamed of having even considered resigning her commitment to Mrs. Johnson, held her hand until the end, eight hours later.

One of God's greatest gifts is the opportunity to have relationships with others. But often, it's easy to forget that along with the opportunity comes a serious responsibility. Those with whom you share a relationship depend on you. That means you stay true to your commitments, even though the going may get tough or you simply may not feel like it. It's not always easy, but God will give you the strength.

TRY THIS: *Think of someone in your community who could use an example of dependability in action. That might mean a commitment to visit regularly, cook a meal a month, baby-sit, or run errands. The possibilities are endless! Just ask and look around. There are many needs to meet. Then just do it, and do it dependably.*

HONEST PEOPLE WILL LEAD A FULL, HAPPY LIFE.

PROVERBS 28:20
GNT

DAVID SAID, MY EYES WILL BE ON THE FAITHFUL IN THE LAND.

PSALM 101:6 NIV

Nothing is more noble, nothing more venerable than fidelity.

CICERO

55

PEACE LIKE A RIVER

Those who counsel peace have joy.

— Proverbs 12:20 NRSV

It was tradition. Each Christmas, members of the women's choir serenaded the church's neighborhood with carols. They practiced their harmonies and, for fun, they wore Dickens-era costumes. Afterward, they met for hot cocoa and a gift exchange.

But this year was different. Before ringing the doorbell at the first house, they heard shouting coming from the inside. As they walked to the next house, three teenagers passed them, arguing and pushing each other. The women turned the corner, only to see a police officer giving a sobriety test to a driver who was shouting obscenities.

The women returned to the church, but they didn't feel much like hot cocoa or gifts. For the first time, they realized how desperately the neighborhood—their world—needed the message of "peace on earth" promised in their carols. They bowed their heads and prayed for the people they had encountered. Then they decided to go out again, this time with a renewed sense of purpose.

At times, it can seem like *peace* is a concept found only in the dictionary. The carolers realized their neighborhood was overrun with conflict. Neighborhoods, cities, states, and countries desperately need peace, and yet it will come only when Christ's saving grace changes the hearts of individuals. You are charged with being a one-woman ambassador of peace to the world.

TRY THIS: *Find a particularly good scripture on the topic of peace—such as Psalm 29:11 or John 14:27. Write out the verse on cards—index or business-card size. Keep these in your purse. When you encounter individuals who seem to greatly need to receive a message of peace, share God's peace by handing them a card.*

A HEART AT PEACE GIVES LIFE TO THE BODY.

PROVERBS 14:30 NIV

GOD IS NOT A GOD OF DISORDER BUT OF PEACE.

1 CORINTHIANS 14:33 NIV

Peace is such a precious jewel that I would give anything for it but truth.

MATTHEW HENRY

The Faithful Woman

Not she with traitorous kiss

her Savior stung,

Not she denied him with unholy tongue;

She, while apostles shrank,

could dangers brave,

Last at the cross

and earliest at the grave.

Eaton Stannard Barrett

et love and faithfulness never leave you; bind them around your neck, write them on the tablet of your heart.

— Proverbs 3:3 GNT

he faithful will abound with blessings.

— Proverbs 28:20 NRSV

GOD DID NOT CALL US TO BE SUCCESSFUL, BUT TO BE FAITHFUL.

MOTHER TERESA

I'm Yours, Lord

Obey the LORD, be humble, and you will get riches, honor, and a long life.

— *Proverbs 22:4* GNT

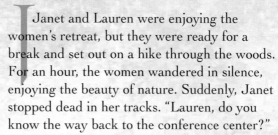

OBEDIENCE TO GOD IS ALWAYS FOR OUR GOOD AND HIS GLORY. —AUTHOR UNKNOWN

Janet and Lauren were enjoying the women's retreat, but they were ready for a break and set out on a hike through the woods. For an hour, the women wandered in silence, enjoying the beauty of nature. Suddenly, Janet stopped dead in her tracks. "Lauren, do you know the way back to the conference center?"

Lost and on the verge of panic, Janet and Lauren wandered around until they spotted a cabin. Relieved, they asked the old man who answered the door for help.

He drew them a rough map, and they set off. But nothing looked familiar, and more than once, they discussed scrapping the map and going on their own instincts. In the end, they decided to obey the directions the old man had given them. They were happy they had done so when they finally saw smoke from the conference center's chimney in the distance.

Obeying God is a difficult, full-time job. Even when you think you know a better way for your life than he does, obedience means doing what he says anyway. It's particularly difficult when you're feeling lost and vulnerable. But have confidence that obedience will take you to the right place, the place God intends for you to be. He always knows what's best for you. Obey him and you will always be able to find your way!

Try This: *On a piece of paper write the following: "Today, [date], I resolve to obey God in every area of my life and follow his instructions as he makes me able." Now sign it and put it in a special place where you will see and acknowledge it often. Read and renew your commitment once a week.*

THOSE WHO OBEY WHAT THEY ARE TAUGHT GUARD THEIR LIVES.

PROVERBS 19:16
NIRV

JESUS SAID, "IF YOU LOVE ME, YOU WILL OBEY WHAT I COMMAND."

JOHN 14:15 NIV

I know the power obedience has of making things easy which seem impossible.

SAINT TERESA OF AVILA

I Can't Believe I Said That

If you want to stay out of trouble, be careful what you say.

~ *Proverbs* 21:23 GNT

Too many of us
speak twice
before we
think.
—Author
Unknown

Jenny thought Claire had already left the hair salon. But she was sitting in the reception area reading magazines and waiting for her husband to pick her up. Unfortunately, Claire was in clear earshot of Jenny's station. When Jenny's next customer came in, she began a monologue about the fashion statement—or rather "misstatement," as Jenny dubbed it—of her previous customer. Jenny prattled on about how the clothes Claire wore just didn't go with her body's shape and how they made her look positively frumpy. "It's too bad," Jenny said. "Claire really has the potential to be cute."

Claire heard every word and was hurt. Jenny, just minutes earlier, had been flattering and full of compliments for her. Now Jenny was disparaging Claire's appearance and mocking her to a stranger.

Weeks later, Jenny wondered why Claire, a faithful customer for five years, never called to make another appointment.

Jenny committed a serious indiscretion with long-lasting consequences. Because of her thoughtless and unkind remarks, she not only lost a good customer, but she also wounded—and probably lost—a friend. Jenny learned a hard lesson, but there is no going back. Once hurtful words leave your mouth, there is no retracting them. It's best never to say things you'll later regret. Make it your habit to keep others' feelings in mind at all times and to think before you speak.

TRY THIS: The next time you see a puddle of water, drop a stone into it. Notice how far the ripples spread out from the center. Careless words also have a ripple effect. Unlike ripples in water, however, the effect goes on and on, never ending. Pray that God will help you avoid damaging your relationships through careless words.

PLEASANT WORDS ARE A HONEYCOMB, SWEET TO THE SOUL AND HEALING TO THE BONES.

PROVERBS 16:24 NIV

THE TONGUE OF THE WISE BRINGS HEALING.

PROVERBS 12:18 NIV

It is easy to utter what has been kept silent, but impossible to recall what has been uttered.

PLUTARCH

Always Unnoticed

All hard work brings a profit.

— *Proverbs 14:23* NIV

Gladys had been the church's cleaning woman for three decades. She sometimes complained about the messes the youth group made and the dirty dishes left after the women's luncheons, but she took her job of caring for God's house seriously.

Gladys also never missed a Sunday service. She sat in the back, ready for action should something need tidying. Of course, nothing ever did, until one Sunday when the pastor called her to the front, saying that he just couldn't preach with dust on his lectern.

Gladys rushed to the podium and was surprised when he presented her with a beautiful new Bible. It was to commemorate her thirty years of service. To a standing ovation, Gladys returned to her seat. She was overcome with emotion. For all those years, she had simply done what she thought God expected of her.

✺ Gladys's unassuming attitude toward the job she had done for years is a wonderful example of the proper attitude toward work. Gladys labored not to get ahead in life or for personal recognition or to make lots of money. She worked for an eternal purpose—to bring glory to God. Consider your attitude toward work. How would you describe it? Whether you hold a regular 9-to-5 job or are working in the home, strive to bring glory to God rather than to yourself in all you do.

✺ TRY THIS: *Imagine yourself receiving a service review, not from your employer, but from God. Ask yourself what would be his assessment of your job performance in such areas as motivation, relationship with coworkers, and attitude. In what ways would he suggest you change your approach to your job? Put it down on paper. Each year, do another review and compare it with the one before.*

DILIGENT HANDS
WILL RULE.

PROVERBS 12:24 NIV

GOD IS FAIR. HE
WILL NOT FORGET
WHAT YOU
HAVE DONE.

HEBREWS 6:10 NIRV

It is not doing the thing which we like to do, but liking to do the thing which we have to do, that makes life blessed.

JOHANN WOLFGANG VON GOETHE

Enough for Today

Trust in the LORD with all your heart. Never rely on what you think you know.

— Proverbs 3:5 GNT

Phyllis had been at the open house all day, and she was happy with the number of people who had dropped by to see the little Victorian house in the country. It was her first listing as a real estate broker, and the day had resulted in a good list of prospective buyers. By the time she was ready to leave, however, it was dark and a deep fog had rolled in.

As Phyllis began her trip back into town over unfamiliar, winding roads, her nervousness grew. The fog enveloped her car. Even with fog lights on, she could see only a few feet ahead. Suddenly a thought occurred to her: If she drove slowly, the distance she could see would be enough. Once she realized that she didn't need to see the entire road ahead, she relaxed. All she had to do was keep her eyes on the few feet of illuminated road in front of her.

Life is a lot like the dark, winding, unfamiliar road. It's often impossible to see what's around the bend, much less what lies more than a few feet ahead. God wants you to trust him to illuminate as much of the road ahead as you need. It's not easy, but with each passing mile your faith will grow and you will become more confident that God will see you safely to your destination.

TRY THIS: *You can't see faith, but you can see its results. The next time you turn on a light, think about the power of your own faith. Is it a 40-watt faith or a 100-watt faith? Each time you flip a light switch, whisper a prayer that God will help you exercise your faith in him so that it grows more and more powerful every day.*

YOUR FAITH, THEN, DOES NOT REST ON HUMAN WISDOM BUT ON GOD'S POWER.

1 CORINTHIANS 2:5
GNT

FAITH IS THE ASSURANCE OF THINGS HOPED FOR, THE CONVICTION OF THINGS NOT SEEN.

HEBREWS 11:1 NRSV

Your faith is what you believe, not what you know.

JOHN LANCASTER SPALDING

The Confident Woman

Always place in God thy trust,

Will and do what's right and true;

Let thy soul be brave and just;

Show thy Lord a humbler mind;

Thou shalt thus his favor find;

Love but few and simple things;

Simple life much comfort brings.

Thomas à Kempis

The LORD will be your confidence.

— *Proverbs 3:26* NIV

The Sovereign LORD, the Holy One of Israel, says to the people, "Come back and quietly trust in me. Then you will be strong and secure."

— *Isaiah 30:15* GNT

CONFIDENCE IN THE NATURAL WORLD IS SELF-RELIANCE, IN THE SPIRITUAL WORLD IT IS GOD-RELIANCE.

OSWALD CHAMBERS

Hanging On

The hopes of good people lead to joy, but wicked people can look forward to nothing.

— *Proverbs 10:28* GNT

Hope can see heaven through the thickest clouds.
—Thomas Benton Brooks

Elizabeth was in the hospital recovering from hip-replacement surgery. The surgery was successful, just as it had been for Elizabeth's roommate, Claudia, who had undergone the same procedure.

However, Elizabeth's recovery was progressing so much more quickly than Claudia's. The difference in their recovery was puzzling to the hospital staff, because the women were the same age and in comparable physical condition. Soon the staff realized that there was one big difference between the two patients. Elizabeth had something to look forward to; Claudia didn't.

Elizabeth revealed that the surgery and painful recovery period were all worthwhile because she and her grandson had agreed they would go horseback riding as soon as she was back on her feet. They had been unable to ride together since her hip had begun to fail a year earlier. To Elizabeth, each day in the hospital was one day closer to realizing her dream. It gave her the hope and courage she needed to recover quickly.

Medical studies consistently find that people who are hopeful are at less risk for disease—and heal more quickly—than those who are not. In these unsettling days, there are many things in the world that can chip away at your hope. But rejoice, God has provided a solid basis for being optimistic about your future. He has given you the hope of salvation through his Son. God invites you daily to claim that hope. The bonus is that it's also good for your health.

Try this: The next time you're outside, stand facing the sun. Then turn and face away from the sun. What difference do you notice? Your shadow appears only when you're not facing the sun. Say a prayer asking God to help you to keep your life always turned toward him so that you can live in hope rather than in the shadows.

There really is hope for you tomorrow.

Proverbs 23:18
NIRV

The LORD takes pleasure in those who fear him, in those who hope in his steadfast love.

Psalm 147:11 NRSV

In hope we count on the possibilities of the future and we do not remain imprisoned in the institutions of the past.

Jürgen Moltmann

71

No Matter What

A kindhearted woman gains respect.

— *Proverbs* 11:16 NIV

The waitress's smile didn't waver, even though it was the second time the man sent his steak back, complaining that it still wasn't cooked right. In fact, all through the meal, the waitress had successfully fielded all the man's complaints—his fork wasn't clean, the vegetables were mushy, she wasn't quick enough in refilling his glass—while maintaining a helpful demeanor.

Judy witnessed the scene and felt sorry for the waitress and irritated with the boorish and insensitive customer who left without leaving a tip.

When Judy asked the waitress how she could be so kind to such a difficult person, the waitress said simply, "It's my job to be kind to all my customers—no matter what." Judy left thinking that even though the waitress hadn't even received a tip for her exceptional attitude, her kindness had afforded her something much more valuable—the respect and admiration of all those who witnessed her situation.

Jesus Christ demonstrated the principle of kindness when he gave his life. Despite the fact that humanity had broken God's laws and sullied the beauty of his creation with sin and selfishness, God poured out his kindness on everyone. When you encounter someone who mistreats you, see it as an opportunity to follow in the footsteps of the Savior by responding with kindness and grace. God's blessing will certainly be poured out on you as you set your heart to walk as Jesus walked.

Try this: *Make an effort to be more conscious of people and situations around you in the course of your everyday life. Raised voices. Snappish actions. Disrespectful looks. Observe instances where the target of these actions responds not in kind but rather with kindness. Think about any insights you may have gleaned, and write your discoveries in your journal.*

KIND WORDS WILL CHEER YOU UP.

PROVERBS 12:25 GNT

BE KIND AND HONEST AND YOU WILL LIVE A LONG LIFE.

PROVERBS 21:21 GNT

Be the living expression of God's kindness: kindness in your face, kindness in your eyes, kindness in your smile, kindness in your warm greeting.

MOTHER TERESA

Guarding Your Health

Obey the LORD and refuse to do wrong. If you do, it will be like good medicine, healing your wounds and easing your pains.

— *Proverbs 3:7–8* GNT

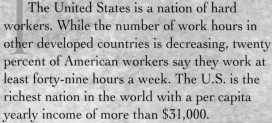

Life is not merely being alive, but being well.
—Marcus Valerius

The United States is a nation of hard workers. While the number of work hours in other developed countries is decreasing, twenty percent of American workers say they work at least forty-nine hours a week. The U.S. is the richest nation in the world with a per capita yearly income of more than $31,000.

However, people can be so intent on getting ahead that they often neglect other, vital aspects of life—including their health. The mind-set of people who are this intent seems to be that there's too much to do and too little time to do it. Over the past twenty years, the obesity rate among American adults has doubled. Diabetes, high blood pressure, heart disease, and stroke are also growing at an alarming rate, due in large part to the lack of attention to such health basics as exercise and diet.

It's ironic that many Americans who sacrifice their health in the pursuit of money eventually end up spending it all on medical care.

༄ God has given a simple formula for a happy life: Maintain a healthy balance, giving proper attention to each vital area, including relationships, finances, spiritual growth, and physical health. One of the quickest ways to destroy happiness is to let one area consume all your time and energy, allowing the others to be neglected. So how's your balancing act? Is one area— such as work—taking over the others? Don't let your health come in last. Remember that your health is one area you can't afford to overlook.

༄ Try this: *Just do it—get out and take a walk, or ride a bike, or go rollerblading. As you are exercising, use the time to talk to God and ask him to help you guard your health. Ask him to help you maintain a proper balance in all areas of your life, giving each aspect the time and attention it deserves.*

Kind words are like honey—sweet to the taste and good for your health.

Proverbs 16:24 GNT

Beloved, I pray that all may go well with you and that you may be in good health.

3 John 2 NRSV

Look at your health; and if you have it praise God, and value it next to a good conscience.

Izaak Walton

75

A Righteous Cause

Speak up for people who cannot speak for themselves. Protect the rights of all who are helpless.

— *Proverbs 31:8 GNT*

Justice is
truth in
action
—Joseph Joubert

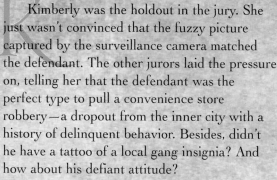

Kimberly was the holdout in the jury. She just wasn't convinced that the fuzzy picture captured by the surveillance camera matched the defendant. The other jurors laid the pressure on, telling her that the defendant was the perfect type to pull a convenience store robbery—a dropout from the inner city with a history of delinquent behavior. Besides, didn't he have a tattoo of a local gang insignia? And how about his defiant attitude?

Kimberly still resisted. She insisted the evidence wasn't there. Regardless of the defendant's past and despite his appearance, she just couldn't go along with the other jurors. The result was a hung jury, and the young man went free. Kimberly knew the other jurors were disappointed in her, but she truly believed she had done the right thing. Fortunately, it wasn't long before the real criminal, who matched the surveillance video without question, was captured. Kimberly thanked God for giving her the courage to see justice done.

Speaking out for justice isn't an easy thing to do. It almost always means going against the majority opinion and enduring the disapproval of others. It's hard, but if you need an example to motivate you, look at Jesus. To defend the cause of justice and do the will of his Father, he stood up to the powerful religious leaders of his day. He understood what it took to do the right thing. And he has promised to give you the strength and courage to follow in his footsteps.

TRY THIS: *Choose a cause you feel strongly about. That cause could be stricter penalties for corporate fraud or jail time for those who continue to drive drunk or any injustice you feel passionately about. Take time to research your cause, and then get involved. Write a letter to your congressperson or volunteer your time to help increase awareness.*

DO WHAT IS RIGHT AND FAIR; THAT PLEASES THE LORD MORE THAN BRINGING HIM SACRIFICES.

PROVERBS 21:3 GNT

IT IS NOT RIGHT TO FAVOR THE GUILTY AND KEEP THE INNOCENT FROM RECEIVING JUSTICE.

PROVERBS 18:5 GNT

True peace is not merely the absence of tension; it is the presence of justice.

MARTIN LUTHER KING, JR.

The Joyous Woman

Joy is a fruit that will not grow

In nature's barren soil;

All we can boast, till Christ we know,

Is vanity and toil.

But where the Lord hath planted grace,

And made His glories known,

These fruits of heavenly joy and peace

Are found, and there alone.

John Newton

Those who work for good will find happiness.

— *Proverbs 12:20* GNT

Be joyful always; pray continually; give thanks in all circumstances.

—*1 Thessalonians 5:16–18* NIV

REAL JOY COMES NOT FROM EASE OR RICHES OR FROM PRAISE OF MEN, BUT FROM DOING SOMETHING WORTHWHILE.

SIR WILFRED GRENFELL

The Rumor Stops Here

No one who gossips can be trusted with a secret, but you can put confidence in someone who is trustworthy.

— Proverbs 11:13 GNT

WHOEVER GOSSIPS TO YOU WILL GOSSIP ABOUT YOU.
—AUTHOR UNKNOWN

On Monday morning, Brenda got a phone call from Mr. Johnson's secretary, who told her to report immediately to his office. Brenda couldn't imagine why she was being called into the office of the employee relations manager. She certainly hadn't done anything that deserved a reprimand.

When she arrived at Mr. Johnson's office, Brenda was surprised to find two of her coworkers already there. Mr. Johnson closed the door and then began to relate to them what had happened. A rumor had been going around the office that Melissa, another employee, might be pregnant since she had been sick at her stomach one morning and had to go home. The rumor had gotten back to Melissa. Being a devoted Christian—and single—she was hurt and embarrassed.

Brenda protested—she had only been on the receiving end of the rumor. But she knew she owed Melissa an apology regardless, because she hadn't done anything to stop the rumor.

It's a truth in life that if there were no tale-hearers, there would be no tale-bearers. And consider this: gossip, which is often based on insufficient or untrue information, rarely lifts anyone up; instead, it spreads unhappiness and leaves hurt in its wake. God's standard requires truth, honesty, and fair dealings. Whenever you're confronted by a gossip session, think about this twist on the Golden Rule—do unto another as if you were the other—then walk away.

Try this: Tomorrow, make a conscious effort to recognize the different guises of gossip in your conversations with others. Humor, concern, helpfulness, and indignation are a few of them. How many others can you add to this list? Prayerfully consider them all and ask God to help you recognize and avoid the temptation to listen or to pass them on.

GOSSIP IS SPREAD BY WICKED PEOPLE; THEY STIR UP TROUBLE AND BREAK UP FRIENDSHIPS.

PROVERBS 16:28 GNT

A GOSSIP CAN NEVER KEEP A SECRET. STAY AWAY FROM PEOPLE WHO TALK TOO MUCH.

PROVERBS 20:19 GNT

The three essential rules when speaking of others are:
Is it true? Is it kind? Is it necessary?

AUTHOR UNKNOWN

A Good Name

If you have to choose between a good reputation and great wealth, choose a good reputation.

~ *Proverbs* 22:1 GNT

LIFE IS FOR ONE
GENERATION, A
GOOD NAME IS
FOREVER.
—ANCIENT PROVERB

Beverly was a talented young businesswoman who went to work for a large software company after college graduation. She quickly built a reputation for being hard working, easy to work with, responsible, and loyal.

At the end of her first year, Beverly was selected for a promotion into upper management. She was not only delighted but also surprised because most of her coworkers had been with the company longer than she had.

Once she settled into her new position, Beverly asked her boss why she had been selected for the promotion. "We wanted someone who would be a self-starter, who needed a minimum of supervision, who would follow through on projects, and who interacted well with others. When we talked to those who worked with you, we felt you had those qualifications." Beverly was gratified to learn that her promotion had been the result of a solid reputation, something she had worked from the first day to built.

Having a reputation as a good employee was the key that opened doors of opportunity for Beverly within the company. Talk and credentials can get a person only so far, and a good reputation cannot be overestimated. If you are eager to move ahead, heed God's Word and make building a strong reputation a priority. Don't bother to try to convince your supervisor how good you are—simply prove it by doing as good a job as possible.

Try this: Try building a house of cards—see how tall you can build it before it falls down. Now build another structure with interlocking pieces rather than flimsy cards. The new structure is strong and can be compared to getting ahead by building on a sturdy foundation of character and good reputation.

A GOOD NAME IS BETTER THAN FINE PERFUME.

ECCLESIASTES 7:1 NIV

THE GOOD OBTAIN FAVOR FROM THE LORD.

PROVERBS 12:2 NRSV

Glass, china, and reputation are easily crack'd and never well mended.

BENJAMIN FRANKLIN

83

Going On

Let God transform you inwardly by a complete change of your mind. Then you will be able to know the will of God—what is good and is pleasing to him and is perfect.

— *Romans 12:2* GNT

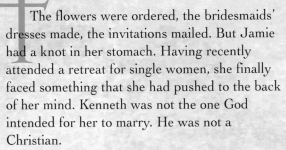

There is precious instruction to be got by finding where we were wrong.
—Thomas Carlyle

The flowers were ordered, the bridesmaids' dresses made, the invitations mailed. But Jamie had a knot in her stomach. Having recently attended a retreat for single women, she finally faced something that she had pushed to the back of her mind. Kenneth was not the one God intended for her to marry. He was not a Christian.

The closer the big day came, the more convinced Jamie became that she had made a mistake agreeing to marry Kenneth. She made the toughest decision of her life three days before the ceremony—she called off the wedding.

Jamie loved Kenneth more than she had ever loved anyone before. But when she took the matter to God in prayer, God convicted her of the wrong decision she had made. She hadn't consulted God before she had let Kenneth court her. She knew now that God was telling her to wait and have the courage to go on because he had something much better in mind for her future. Jamie felt terrible about how she had ignored God and hurt Kenneth.

It's human to make mistakes. The real problem comes when you allow those mistakes to take you in the wrong direction. Once you start down a certain road, it's difficult to admit that you are going the wrong way and then turn around. But regardless of how difficult turning around may be, you will never be sorry when you choose to correct your mistakes rather than to compound them. God is always there to give you the courage you need to set a new path and go on.

TRY THIS: *Draw a line down the center of a piece of paper. On the left, note a mistake you've recently made. On the right, note what you learned from that mistake. Now cross out the mistake and praise God for the lesson you learned. At the same time, ask God to help you avoid such mistakes in the future.*

IF YOU LISTEN TO ADVICE AND ARE WILLING TO LEARN, ONE DAY YOU WILL BE WISE.

PROVERBS 19:20 GNT

LEARN PRUDENCE; ACQUIRE INTELLIGENCE, YOU WHO LACK IT.

PROVERBS 8:5 NRSV

Learn from the mistakes of others — you can't live long enough to make them all yourself.

MARTIN VANBEE

The Lord Gives Me Strength

The LORD protects honest people.

— Proverbs 10:29 GNT

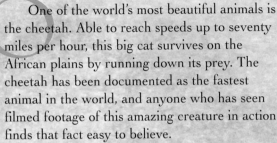

> YOU BECOME
> STRONGER ONLY
> WHEN YOU
> BECOME WEAKER.
> —Erwin W. Lutzer

One of the world's most beautiful animals is the cheetah. Able to reach speeds up to seventy miles per hour, this big cat survives on the African plains by running down its prey. The cheetah has been documented as the fastest animal in the world, and anyone who has seen filmed footage of this amazing creature in action finds that fact easy to believe.

However, the cheetah cannot sustain its incredibly fast speed for very long. That's because its heart is disproportionately small for the tremendous physical exertion. For the cheetah's muscles to sustain speed, they must be constantly supplied with great amounts of oxygen, delivered by the blood. The cheetah's small heart simply cannot pump enough blood to sustain the oxygen demand of its muscles. So it tires quickly.

It's a fact that unless the cheetah can capture its prey in the first burst of speed, it must abandon the chase and try again another time.

People can be like cheetahs—starting projects with great enthusiasm, but then petering out. Whether it's something as trivial as cleaning closets or as important as maintaining a daily devotional time, human stamina at times simply can't keep us going. The things that God has laid on your heart to do are important to him, however, and he will back your strength with his when your endurance comes up short. Ask God to give you his strength today to carry out his will.

Try this: If you were to pick up a heavy object, it wouldn't be long before your muscles got tired. Next time you need to lift something heavy, ask someone to help, and see how much longer you are able to hold it. God does that for you as well; he gives you his strength to help you hold on. You can rely on God in whatever you do.

YOU WILL RECEIVE THE STRENGTH YOU NEED WHEN YOU STAY CALM AND TRUST IN ME.

ISAIAH 30:15 NIRV

I HAVE THE STRENGTH TO FACE ALL CONDITIONS BY THE POWER THAT CHRIST GIVES ME.

PHILIPPIANS 4:13 GNT

Nothing is so strong as gentleness: nothing so gentle as real strength.

SAINT FRANCIS DE SALES

The Good Woman

Do all the good you can,

By all the means you can,

In all the ways you can,

In all the places you can,

At all the times you can,

To all the people you can,

As long as ever you can,

In the end results in glory.

John Wesley

Do not withhold good from those who deserve it.

— *Proverbs 3:27 NIV*

You will earn the trust and respect of others if you work for good.

— *Proverbs 14:22 GNT*

THE LEAST ACT OF TRUE GOODNESS IS INDEED THE BEST PROOF OF THE EXISTENCE OF GOD.

JACQUES MARITAIN

Making It Big

Commit to the LORD whatever you do, and your plans will succeed.

~ Proverbs 16:3 NIV

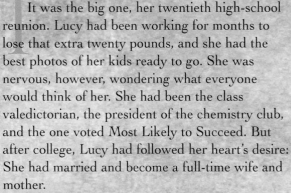

It was the big one, her twentieth high-school reunion. Lucy had been working for months to lose that extra twenty pounds, and she had the best photos of her kids ready to go. She was nervous, however, wondering what everyone would think of her. She had been the class valedictorian, the president of the chemistry club, and the one voted Most Likely to Succeed. But after college, Lucy had followed her heart's desire: She had married and become a full-time wife and mother.

At the reunion, Lucy was impressed by her classmates. Sandy was a gifted defense lawyer. Jan was doing great work as a medical research scientist. Cheri had published two novels. Given her friends' impressive achievements, Lucy was surprised when they, in turn, expressed genuine admiration for Lucy's accomplishments—a successful marriage and happy, healthy children.

Instead of feeling like an underachiever, Lucy left the reunion feeling grateful to God that he had blessed her with so much success in life.

❧ If you were to ask one of your friends to share her secrets to success with you, no doubt it would make interesting conversation. But your friend's formulas may not necessarily be applicable to your life. How she achieved success doesn't matter. What does matter is God's formula for success, spelled out in Proverbs 16:3. The formula is this: Talk to God, seek his will, ask him to bless your plans, and then commit them to his care and direction for success in carrying them out.

❧ TRY THIS: *Write down your plans for this year. Note three things that you hope to accomplish in those twelve months. Then ask yourself these questions: Are my plans God-approved? Have I turned them over to his direction? If the answers are no, commit your plans to him. You can be sure that God wants you to succeed in the things he wills.*

PLANS FAIL FOR LACK OF COUNSEL, BUT WITH MANY ADVISERS THEY SUCCEED.

PROVERBS 15:22 NIV

MAY THE LORD GIVE YOU THE DESIRE OF YOUR HEART AND MAKE ALL YOUR PLANS SUCCEED.

PSALM 20:4 NIV

It is surprising to observe how much more anybody may become by simply always being in His place.

AUTHOR UNKNOWN

Wise Solutions

Sensible people always think before they act.

~ *Proverbs* 13:16 GNT

THERE IS
NOTHING MORE
UNCOMMON
THAN COMMON
SENSE.
—FRANK LLOYD
WRIGHT

Nan had risen to the top quickly in the corporation. And no wonder. She had a knack for spotting problems and coming up with solutions that made perfect sense. Even situations that had others completely baffled were no match for her uncanny insight. In fact, after conversations with Nan, people often said, "Why didn't I think of that myself?"

Early one morning, the president of the company came to see Nan. Her assistant politely told him that Nan had asked not to be disturbed. But after hesitating for a few moments, he opened the door and entered Nan's office anyway. There he found Nan on her knees, praying.

The president quietly backed out and closed the door. He asked Nan's assistant, "Does she do this often?" The assistant responded, "Yes, every morning at this time."

As he turned to walk away, he said, "No wonder everyone comes to her for advice."

Common sense has been defined as wisdom dressed in work clothes. It's not uncommon to encounter someone who always seems to have the right solution for any situation. That person is putting wisdom to work. God is the source of all wisdom—common sense, too—and he says in the Bible that he will give wisdom to anyone who asks for it. If you have found yourself longing for the kind of common sense that can help you find solutions in life, just ask God for it.

Try this: If a situation in your life has you baffled and just can't seem to be resolved, ask God to give you his "wisdom in work clothes" for dealing with your immediate concern as well as future problems that arise. At the same time, make an appointment to talk it over with someone you respect—someone who always has good common sense.

SENSIBLE PEOPLE ACCEPT GOOD ADVICE.

PROVERBS 10:8 GNT

SENSIBLE PEOPLE WILL SEE TROUBLE COMING AND AVOID IT.

PROVERBS 22:3 GNT

Fine sense and exalted sense are not half so useful as common sense.

ALEXANDER POPE

Hands Extended

Be generous and share your food with the poor. You will be blessed for it.

— Proverbs 22:9 GNT

During the Great Depression, hobos wandering from place to place searching for a free meal or a short-term job were a common sight. In fact, there were so many of them, they developed a system of graffiti symbols to communicate specific messages with one another.

For example, a simple sketch of a cat drawn on the sidewalk or a fence by a house told other hobos that "a kind-hearted woman lives here," a woman who was quick to offer a meal or a glass of lemonade to anyone down on his luck who knocked on her door.

The days of the hobo are gone, but the need for hospitable women who will generously share with others is not. Hobos may not be knocking at your door looking for a free meal, but plenty of people in your life would appreciate a hand extended in welcome.

With all the magazine articles and television shows setting forth how to be the perfect hostess, it's easy to feel inadequate. According to them, opening your home to others involves a great deal of energy and social savvy. But first-class hospitality is more than folding napkins into unusual shapes or learning techniques for stunning presentation or making the perfect cup of coffee. It is the offering of warmth and the extending of genuine Christian affection to others.

TRY THIS: *Think of a friend that you haven't spent time with lately, and invite her over to your home for lunch or dinner. Prepare for her visit and treat her as you would an angel in disguise. This means spending more time demonstrating genuine interest in her and her life than worrying about how you rate as a hostess.*

OPEN YOUR HOMES TO EACH OTHER WITHOUT COMPLAINING.

1 PETER 4:9 GNT

REMEMBER TO WELCOME STRANGERS IN YOUR HOMES. THERE WERE SOME WHO DID THAT AND WELCOMED ANGELS WITHOUT KNOWING IT.

HEBREWS 13:2 GNT

What is there more kindly than the feeling between host and guest?

AESCHYLUS

BACK TO THE BOOKS

When you stop learning, you will soon neglect what you already know.

— *Proverbs 19:27* GNT

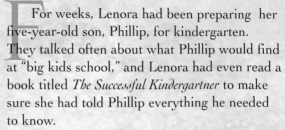

LEARNING IS ITS
OWN EXCEEDING
GREAT REWARD.
—WILLIAM HAZLITT

For weeks, Lenora had been preparing her five-year-old son, Phillip, for kindergarten. They talked often about what Phillip would find at "big kids school," and Lenora had even read a book titled *The Successful Kindergartner* to make sure she had told Phillip everything he needed to know.

Phillip shed no tears when Lenora dropped him off on the first day of school. And that evening at dinner, he couldn't say enough about his day. He told Lenora all about the other kids, the teacher, and the playground equipment. *All that preparation certainly paid off*, Lenora thought as she tucked her sleepy boy into bed.

The next morning, Lenora woke Phillip in plenty of time for a hearty breakfast before his second day of kindergarten. Rubbing his eyes, Phillip looked at Lenora with confusion. "It's time to get ready for school," she said. She was surprised when he responded innocently, "But I just went yesterday."

In all her preparation, Lenora forgot to let Phillip in on the fact that school is a daily thing. Even when formal schooling is long a part of the past, however, learning still takes place daily. Continuing to learn and grow are important. Not only has medical research connected life-long learning to the prevention of such brain conditions as Alzheimer's disease and age-related dementia, but God wants you to continually learn and grow in your understanding of what it means to follow him.

TRY THIS: *Learn something new. In any community, there are many opportunities to be exposed to new subjects—community college classes, Bible study classes, parks and recreation workshops, discussion groups, and so forth. Check out the learning opportunities near you. Keep in mind that you don't have to know anything about the subject to begin at the entry level—the door is wide open.*

IF YOU REFUSE TO LEARN, YOU ARE HURTING YOURSELF. IF YOU ACCEPT CORRECTION, YOU WILL BECOME WISER

PROVERBS 15:32 GNT

APPLY YOUR MIND TO INSTRUCTION AND YOUR EAR TO WORDS OF KNOWLEDGE.

PROVERBS 23:12 NRSV

Unless we accept lifelong learning as a habit, we're shortening our lives.

AUTHOR UNKNOWN

The Happy Woman

It takes so little to make us glad;

Just a cheering clasp

of a friendly hand,

Just a word from one

who can understand;

And we finish the task

we long had planned

And we lose the doubt

and the fear we had—

So little it takes to make us glad.

Author Unknown

Trust in the LORD and you will be happy.

~ *Proverbs* 16:20 GNT

God gives wisdom, knowledge, and happiness to those who please him.

~ *Ecclesiastes* 2:26 GNT

It is not how much we have, but how much we enjoy, that makes happiness.

Author Unknown

THE REAL REASON

You may think that everything you do is right, but remember that the LORD judges your motives.

— *Proverbs 21:2* GNT

Man sees your actions, but God your motives.
—Thomas à Kempis

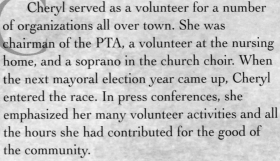

Cheryl served as a volunteer for a number of organizations all over town. She was chairman of the PTA, a volunteer at the nursing home, and a soprano in the church choir. When the next mayoral election year came up, Cheryl entered the race. In press conferences, she emphasized her many volunteer activities and all the hours she had contributed for the good of the community.

When Cheryl lost the election to the incumbent, no one was really surprised. The incumbent mayor had been the favorite all along. But everyone was surprised when Cheryl suddenly resigned her volunteer positions. Soon she wasn't involved in any of the activities she had indicated she was so committed to in campaign speeches. When a friend asked Cheryl why she made such a dramatic change, she said, "I thought those things would help me win the election. Since I lost, what's the point?"

꧁ Why—really—do you do the things you do for others? If you are hoping to look good to someone else, receive some type of reward, acquire control over others, or alleviate guilt, it could be that you need to step back and ask God to help you purify your motives. When the motives behind your actions are pleasing to God, your efforts will produce good things—eternal things—in your life and the lives of others.

꧁ TRY THIS: *Write a list of the last five actions you took on behalf of another person or cause. Now take an honest look at each of those actions. Write down all of your reasons for undertaking the action. Some of your motives will become clear right away; others will become clearer as you pray about them.*

YOU MAY THINK EVERYTHING YOU DO IS RIGHT, BUT THE LORD JUDGES YOUR MOTIVES.

PROVERBS 16:2 GNT

THE LORD KNOWS ALL OUR THOUGHTS AND DESIRES.

1 CHRONICLES 28:9 GNT

One of the most excellent intentions that we can possibly have in all our actions is to do them because our Lord did them.

SAINT FRANCIS DE SALES

I'm Happy for You

Peace of mind makes the body healthy.

— *Proverbs 14:30* GNT

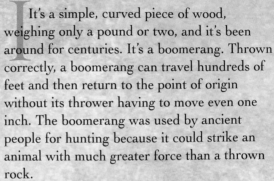

Envy is the art of counting the other fellow's blessings instead of your own.
—Harold Coffin

It's a simple, curved piece of wood, weighing only a pound or two, and it's been around for centuries. It's a boomerang. Thrown correctly, a boomerang can travel hundreds of feet and then return to the point of origin without its thrower having to move even one inch. The boomerang was used by ancient people for hunting because it could strike an animal with much greater force than a thrown rock.

In your life, jealousy can work much like a boomerang. It can cause you to fling hurtful words and actions toward others. Those words and actions can come back to you, polluting your thoughts and hardening your heart.

Don't allow yourself to become discontented when you see the good fortune of others. Turn your back on envious thoughts and replace them with thoughts of thankfulness and good will. Then send out words of congratulations and rejoicing. Let the boomerang effect return to you with good things.

It's easy to feel that everyone else has a better life than you do. But letting that feeling draw you into jealous thoughts will only make you feel worse. Instead, replace those thoughts with prayers of thanksgiving to God for what he has given you, and send up a prayer that God will continue to bless those you are tempted to envy.

TRY THIS: *The next time you feel jealous of anyone, go to God in prayer and ask him to keep you from temptation. Add the person's name to your prayer list on or near the top. Pray at least once a day that God will continue to pour out his richest blessings on that person. Pray it until it comes from your heart.*

WHERE THERE IS JEALOUSY AND SELFISHNESS, THERE IS ALSO DISORDER AND EVERY KIND OF EVIL.

JAMES 3:16 GNT

ANGER IS CRUEL AND DESTRUCTIVE, BUT IT IS NOTHING COMPARED TO JEALOUSY.

PROVERBS 27:4 GNT

Envy takes the joy, happiness, and contentment out of living.
BILLY GRAHAM

It's a Choice

The cheerful heart has a continual feast.

— *Proverbs* 15:15 NIV

CHEERFULNESS,
LIKE SPRING,
OPENS ALL THE
BLOSSOMS OF THE
INWARD MAN.
—JEAN PAUL
RICHTER

When Mrs. Snyder's husband died, she realized that his life insurance would be inadequate to allow her to stay in their home. Less than a month after the funeral, she had to sell and move into a small apartment.

Mrs. Snyder had lost her husband and her home. In shock and grief, she prayed to God for strength and mustered her inner spiritual reserves to go on. Her new neighbors at the apartment complex felt sorry for her when they heard her story and expected to meet a woman who was depressed and overcome with sadness. They were amazed to make the acquaintance of a woman who managed to be smiling and cheerful despite her recent tragedies.

An apartment neighbor finally asked Mrs. Snyder how she managed to maintain such a cheerful attitude. She said, "God is with me every minute of every day. He has given me the strength to choose to live a happy life."

Mrs. Snyder knew a secret: cheerfulness is a choice. No matter what happens to you, you can choose how to react to it. Even the worst life experience can be met with a positive attitude and a determination to find the good that God can bring from it. As God was creating the world, he pronounced each day, without exception, as good. You can do the same with each day of your life. God will help you choose cheerfulness.

TRY THIS: *"Have a nice day" is a common phrase. The next time someone tells you to have a nice day, thank him or her and consider their words a reminder that it is totally up to you whether your day will be nice or not. Then say a prayer asking God to help you choose cheerfulness.*

WHEN PEOPLE ARE HAPPY, THEY SMILE.

PROVERBS 15:13 GNT

BEING CHEERFUL KEEPS YOU HEALTHY. IT IS SLOW DEATH TO BE GLOOMY ALL THE TIME.

PROVERBS 17:22 GNT

Everyone must have felt that a cheerful friend is like a sunny day, which sheds its brightness on all around.

Sir John Lubbock

I'll Get to It Later

The plans of people who work hard will succeed.

~ *Proverbs* 21:5 NIRV

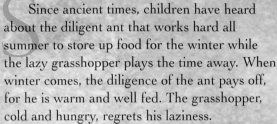

Patience and
diligence, like
faith, remove
mountains.
—William Penn

Since ancient times, children have heard about the diligent ant that works hard all summer to store up food for the winter while the lazy grasshopper plays the time away. When winter comes, the diligence of the ant pays off, for he is warm and well fed. The grasshopper, cold and hungry, regrets his laziness.

In truth, ants are diligent creatures. Even if you brush them off the picnic table, it's not long before they're back, lured by your fried chicken and potato salad. Have you ever seen ants taking a break? They seem always to be moving. They don't seem disturbed by the size of the job, and they often tackle objects twice their size and haul them back to the nest. Indeed, for thousands of years ants have been providing a great natural lesson about the value of diligence and hard work.

As the lowly ant demonstrates, life is a roll-up-your-sleeves proposition. God gives you the basic ingredients you need for your daily bread, but he expects you to do the baking. You can have lots of enthusiasm for the final product—a warm, tasty loaf of bread—but unless you are willing to do the work required to produce it, enthusiasm won't get you very far. When it comes to the tasks that lay ahead, roll up your sleeves and get to work.

TRY THIS: *Write the following saying on a sticky note and place it where you'll see it often, such as on the bathroom mirror or on car dashboard or by the kitchen sink: "The best time to get something done is between yesterday and tomorrow." Read it out loud to yourself.*

HARD WORK WILL GIVE YOU POWER; BEING LAZY WILL MAKE YOU A SLAVE.

PROVERBS 12:24 GNT

HARD WORK WILL MAKE YOU RICH.

PROVERBS 10:4 GNT

For the diligent the week has seven todays; for the slothful seven tomorrows.

AUTHOR UNKNOWN

The Blessed Woman

The best things are nearest:

Breath in your nostrils,

Light in your eyes,

Flowers at your feet,

Duties at your hand,

The path of God just before you.

Robert Louis Stevenson

The Lord richly blesses everyone who calls on him.

~ *Romans 10:12* NIRV

Good people will receive blessings.

~ *Proverbs 10:6* GNT

Those blessings are sweet that are won with prayers and worn with thanks.

Thomas Goodwin

Straight Talk

Friends mean well, even when they hurt you.

— *Proverbs* 27:6 GNT

THE BETTER
FRIENDS YOU ARE,
THE STRAIGHTER
YOU CAN TALK.
—Saint Francis
Xavier

Jane was excited. She finally landed the job interview for which she had been hoping and praying for. Bonnie, Jane's best friend, agreed to go shopping with her for the perfect outfit to wear for the big event. After spending all morning going from store to store, Jane finally found a suit that she loved. It was bright purple—her favorite color—and had a short skirt that showed off her legs.

I'll take it was on Jane's tongue when Bonnie cleared her throat and shook her head. "That shade of purple really isn't your color," Bonnie said. "And I think the skirt is too short for a job interview."

Jane was a little annoyed by Bonnie's remarks, but she heeded the advice. Later that day, Jane found a suit that she liked and Bonnie agreed that it was both flattering and appropriate, Jane gave her best friend a big hug. "You're the best friend in the world," she said. "Thanks for being honest with me."

Friendship is more than pats on the back and nice words. Cherish those friends who tell you what you need to hear rather than just what you want to hear. Their words may be something as simple as helping you choose the right outfit or as complex as being truthful with you about a relationship or an unhealthy habit. Ask God to help you listen to what your friends say, and be willing to return the favor when your friends need your honesty.

Try this: *On a card, write the following words, "You are my cherished friend. I want and need your honesty." Give the card to your most trusted friend. Take the time to discuss the idea of honesty in friendship with her, which will deepen your relationship.*

THE RIGHTEOUS PERSON IS A GUIDE TO HIS FRIEND.

PROVERBS 12:26 GNT

SOME FRIENDSHIPS DO NOT LAST, BUT SOME FRIENDS ARE MORE LOYAL THAN BROTHERS.

PROVERBS 18:24 GNT

Only your real friends will tell you when your face is dirty.
SICILIAN PROVERB

Turning the Other Cheek

Don't take it on yourself to repay a wrong. Trust the LORD and he will make it right.

— *Proverbs* 20:22 GNT

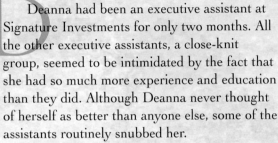

The smallest revenge will poison the soul.
—Jewish Proverb

Deanna had been an executive assistant at Signature Investments for only two months. All the other executive assistants, a close-knit group, seemed to be intimidated by the fact that she had so much more experience and education than they did. Although Deanna never thought of herself as better than anyone else, some of the assistants routinely snubbed her.

Shortly after her first year at Signature, Deanna was promoted to the position of manager. She now found herself supervising those who had treated her badly. She had opportunity to get even, but she didn't. Instead, she talked to God about the situation. Then she made an effort to treat her employees with respect and fairness. She evaluated them fairly on their performance reviews, asked for their input, and praised them for work well done.

Deanna was wise enough to recognize that the temporary feeling of satisfaction she might receive from getting even would cause her more trouble than it was worth.

When you find yourself in a situation where you are being treated badly by someone, talk to God about it. Then release your frustration and ask him to help you find positive ways to deal with your situation. Be sure to treat everyone, regardless of how that person has treated you, with respect and fairness. Break the chain of retribution by setting a new positive standard of personal relations that will build bridges rather than fences.

Try this: *Write out the following prayer: "Heavenly Father, give me the strength I need to place this situation with _____ in your hands. Keep me from the temptation to seek revenge and show me ways to bless and encourage _____." Don't write in the name of the person who is mistreating you. Just speak it into the blank places as you pray.*

DO NOT PAY BACK EVIL WITH EVIL OR CURSING WITH CURSING; INSTEAD, PAY BACK WITH A BLESSING.

1 Peter 3:9 GNT

IF SOMEONE HAS DONE YOU WRONG, DO NOT REPAY HIM WITH A WRONG.

Romans 12:17 GNT

The only people with whom you should try to get even are those who have helped you.

JOHN E. SOUTHARD

CLEAN BEFORE THE LORD

Sometimes it takes a painful experience to make us change our ways.

— *Proverbs* 20:30 GNT

THE PURSUIT OF
HOLINESS IS A
JOINT VENTURE
BETWEEN GOD
AND MAN.
—JERRY BRIDGES

What would you do if you were assigned a tract of prairie land in the Midwest and asked to make it thrive? Would you plant some grass seed? Would you irrigate it? You might be surprised to know that one of the best things you could do for the land is start a fire. Burned ground looks as if there is no life left. But burning stimulates the growth of grasses and other plants, returns nutrients to the soil, and exposes the area to nurturing sunlight.

Unless you're a farmer or a land conservationist, the idea of burning the land to make it thrive probably sounds wrong to you. Like intentional grass fires, the ways of God also often go against conventional human insight. As you allow God to do his work in your life, you will experience the delight of spiritual growth. Open up the fields of your heart and life to his cleansing fire.

God loves you, and he wants you to grow and thrive spiritually. That can happen if you're willing to open your heart completely and honestly to him. He can clean your life by seeking out and sweeping away even the tiniest traces of sin. Even when you don't understand the work he is doing, set your human insights aside. Trust him as his cleansing fire brings a new growth of holiness in your life.

TRY THIS: *The next time you clean the stains from a coffee cup or the kitchen sink, think about what the process requires. Sometimes it requires a scouring pad or a harsh cleanser, like bleach. But the result is a sparkling clean surface. Pray that God will use whatever methods he feels are necessary to make your heart sparkling clean before him.*

JESUS SAID, "THOSE WHOM I LOVE I REBUKE AND DISCIPLINE."

REVELATION 3:19 NIV

NO DISCIPLINE SEEMS PLEASANT AT THE TIME. . . . LATER ON, HOWEVER, IT PRODUCES A HARVEST OF RIGHTEOUSNESS AND PEACE.

HEBREWS 12:11 NIV

Holiness does not consist in doing uncommon things, but in doing every thing with purity of heart.

CARDINAL HENRY E. MANNING

Knowing What to Do

Get all the advice you can, and you will succeed; without it you will fail.
~ *Proverbs 15:22* GNT

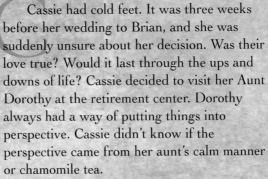

No gift is more precious than good advice.
—Desiderius Erasmus

Cassie had cold feet. It was three weeks before her wedding to Brian, and she was suddenly unsure about her decision. Was their love true? Would it last through the ups and downs of life? Cassie decided to visit her Aunt Dorothy at the retirement center. Dorothy always had a way of putting things into perspective. Cassie didn't know if the perspective came from her aunt's calm manner or chamomile tea.

At the center, Cassie was disappointed to find Dorothy busy playing dominoes with three other ladies. But when they told her to pull up a chair, she did. Amid the clack of dominoes, the women shared stories from their lives and marriages, some funny, some poignant. Cassie was impressed by their wisdom and insight into life, and by the end of the afternoon, she felt better about her marriage. Through their real-life stories and practical advice, the women had given her the assurance she needed to go forward with her decision to become Brian's wife.

Wise advice can come from many sources. The key is being open to receive it. You have probably noticed it's easy to go ahead with your plans without consulting anyone. After all, there's always the chance you might hear something that goes against what you've already made up your mind to do. However, it's good to keep in mind that seeking out and heeding wise advice in the beginning often can prevent trouble later.

TRY THIS: *The next time you find yourself struggling with a decision, think of three people who might be able to give you sound advice. Then have an open mind and an open heart when you ask. After each visit, write down what you learned.*

WISE PEOPLE LISTEN TO ADVICE.

PROVERBS 12:15 GNT

LISTEN TO ADVICE AND ACCEPT INSTRUCTION, THAT YOU MAY GAIN WISDOM FOR THE FUTURE.

PROVERBS 19:20 NRSV

Discuss your affairs with one who is wise and who fears God.

THOMAS À KEMPIS

The Righteous Woman

No condemnation now I dread,

Jesus, and all in him, is mine;

Alive in him, my living Head,

And clothed in righteousness divine,

Bold I approach the eternal throne,

And claim the crown,

through Christ, my own.

Charles Wesley

The LORD *blesses the abode of the righteous.*

— *Proverbs* 3:33 NRSV

You must put on the new self, which is created in God's likeness and reveals itself in the true life that is upright and holy.

— *Ephesians* 4:24 GNT

THE MOST IMPORTANT INGREDIENT OF RIGHTEOUSNESS IS TO RENDER TO GOD THE SERVICE AND HOMAGE DUE TO HIM.

JOHN CALVIN

An Uplifting Word

May our Lord Jesus Christ himself and God our Father . . . encourage you and strengthen you to always do and say what is good.

— *2 Thessalonians 2:16–17* GNT

Encouragement costs you nothing to give, but it is priceless to receive.
—Author Unknown

Have you ever seen geese flying in formation? As you probably know, geese fly this way for a reason. As each goose flaps its wings, it creates an uplift for the one following it. Flying together in this way allows the birds to travel much farther than they could fly on their own. When the lead goose gets tired, it simply rotates to another position in the formation, and another goose takes over. Surprisingly, the honking you hear from a flock of geese is actually encouragement for the ones in the lead to keep up their speed.

What a beautiful illustration of what God intended us to be to one another—supportive, encouraging, and helping to lighten the load of others so they can rest and regain their strength. Ask God to make you an encourager by giving you a good word for someone who is tempted to quit or an act of kindness for someone who has grown cynical.

Uplifting words and actions can be powerful tools in the hand of God. With them, he can encourage a weary soul or bring a wayward heart to repentance. He can restore a life or fulfill a long-forgotten dream. God could do those things without you, but he chooses to use human lips and human hands to deliver comfort and encouragement. In that way, he ensures that two people will be strengthened and uplifted—the giver and the receiver.

Try this: *Choose five people with whom you share a relationship—a friend, a spouse, a sibling, or a coworker, for example. Make it a point in the coming week to write a note of encouragement to each of those people, mentioning with appreciation at least one specific thing that makes that person special.*

A WORD FITLY SPOKEN IS LIKE APPLES OF GOLD IN A SETTING OF SILVER.

PROVERBS 25:11
NRSV

ENCOURAGE THE TIMID, HELP THE WEAK, BE PATIENT WITH EVERYONE.

1 THESSALONIANS 5:14 GNT

More people fail for lack of encouragement than for any other reason.

AUTHOR UNKNOWN

Thinking to Win

The thoughts of the righteous are just.

— *Proverbs 12:5 NRSV*

Our life is
what our
thoughts
make it.
—Catherine of
Siena

Vicky had been on a diet exactly two days, four hours, and twenty-five minutes. She was standing in front of the open refrigerator door for the fifth time today, just staring. She didn't see the celery sticks or nonfat yogurt. She saw the cream cheese and Dr Pepper. It seemed that everywhere she turned, she was bombarded by visions of rich desserts and crispy, brown fried foods.

All Vicky thought about all day was food. She even dreamed about at night. So it was inevitable that Vicky's thoughts would finally overcome her willpower. In the middle of Day 5, she gave in. But she didn't give up. Instead she asked God to help her take charge of her thoughts and focus them on positive things. Then she began again. What Vicky couldn't do alone, she accomplished with God's help.

⁂ Your thoughts are powerful. In truth, every one of your actions starts with a thought. That's why it's important to make your thoughts work for you rather than against you. With God's help, you can discipline your thoughts to benefit your health, your relationships, your work skills, any area of your life. You can allow your thoughts to build you up or tear you down. Commit your thoughts to God and let him show you how to become a winner.

⁂ TRY THIS: *Consciously counter one thought with another. Write down the unproductive thought: "This is too hard. I can't do it." Ask yourself what it contains—worry, fear, failure? Then compose a thought filled with the opposite—faith, safety, success. Productive thought: "I can do this with God as my helper." Each time you encounter the unproductive thought, repeat its positive opposite several times.*

FILL YOUR MINDS
WITH THOSE THINGS
THAT ARE GOOD AND
THAT DESERVE
PRAISE.

PHILIPPIANS 4:8 GNT

A TRANQUIL MIND
GIVES LIFE TO
THE FLESH.

PROVERBS 14:30
NRSV

Change your thoughts and you change your world.
NORMAN VINCENT PEALE

The Wise Woman

Hold on to your wisdom and insight.
Never let them get away from you.
They will provide you with life—
a pleasant and happy life.
You can go safely on your way
and never even stumble.
You will not be afraid
when you go to bed,
and you will sleep soundly
through the night.

Proverbs 3:21–24 GNT

It is better—much better—to have wisdom and knowledge than gold and silver.

— *Proverbs* 16:16 GNT

The law of the LORD is perfect; it gives new strength. The commands of the LORD are trustworthy, giving wisdom to those who lack it.

— *Psalm* 19:7 GNT

KNOWLEDGE IS THE POWER OF THE MIND, WISDOM IS THE POWER OF THE SOUL.

JULIE SHANNAHAN

Other books in the Proverbs for Life™ series:

Proverbs for Life™ for Men
Proverbs for Life™ for Teens
Proverbs for Life™ for You

All available from your favorite bookstore.
We would like to hear from you.
Please send your comments about this book to:

Inspirio™, the gift group of Zondervan
Attn: Product Development
Grand Rapids, Michigan 49530

www.inspirio.com

<u>Our mission:</u>
*To provide distinctively Christian gifts that point people to God's Word
through refreshing messages and innovative designs.*

inspirio™

The gift group of Zondervan